Robert C. Jones

ROBERT C. JONES

BY JOHN BOYLAN

Francine Seders Gallery, Seattle
in association with
University of Washington Press, Seattle and London

Robert Jones: The Life of the Elemental

As a painter, Bob Jones lives in a spare, boiled-down world of dark, elemental shapes, vibrant and complex color, and constant experiment, most often operating within a highly specific structure and a clear focus.

A careful look at his paintings brings to the fore the extent to which painting of a certain sort becomes a contract between the artist and the viewer. It is an unconscious contract that the artist writes, a contract that is inherent in the work itself, a contract that viewers sign in agreeing to look at a painting, really look, instead of engaging in a museum flyby. For those who agree to sign, the contract stipulates that they will consider certain issues of art, matters of form, light, and looking, issues that the artist has chosen, and that they will do so on the artist's terms. What they take away from that experience is up to them, but it will always be informed by the terms of that contract.

Not all painting is so ironclad; much ventures forth more freely, in an anarchic dance, with considerably less expectation of the specific points of art that the audience will confront. But for artists like Jones, who have spent much of their careers examining fundamental concepts of art, the painting becomes the contract, demanding to be seen on its own terms, or not at all.

For a good part of four decades, Jones has brought himself to think clearly and persistently about a small but universal set of issues: issues of form and line, of the way in which color behaves, of how a painting most directly creates a presence. They are what forms the core of abstract painting; however, as he has pursued them, Jones has given them his own twist. His work has

Untitled, 1999 (plate 15, detail)

varied widely over the years, but it has always returned to a specific set of questions, a certain vocabulary. Like a mathematician worrying an elusive proof or a detective with an eye always out for a certain fugitive, Jones has never strayed far from his quest. It is not that he has been looking for answers; more it has been a search for better questions.

At the center of those questions is a fascination with the geometry of composition, the nature of line—its construction and its destruction, its strength and weakness—and the interplay between drawing and painting. Jones can't forget the essential question of painting: It is and must be about seeing clearly, about revealing a distilled sensibility, about capturing light. That's what continues to make it so important.

Several recent paintings are good examples of the language that Jones is speaking, of the issues that he confronts: the focus of his own contract. To begin to enter into that contract, one must start with his long love affair with black.

Jones has a warm, rich palette, reminiscent of Impressionist landscape, but the large expanses of black that have long marked his drawings have also played a significant role in his paintings as well. Both black and white function as colors in themselves, but black is more than that. In plate 15, for example, Jones anchors the painting with arching areas of black. All that happens in the work does so within and around this arch. The strip of warm color on the left of the painting acts in relation to the black, setting up an imbalance, setting up the black, which covers most of the painting, as a distinct form within the canvas. The oval shapes that are etched into the black in turn create their own balance, along with a call and response to the rough black ovals that lie in the warm field within the arch.

More than other colors, the black obscures the loose compositional grid that is at the foundation of many of the paintings that Jones makes. However, it also interacts with what remains of the grid in ways that the other colors cannot. The inner lines of the arch, as survivors of the grid, are softer than the color they contain, so that the role of line changes from one of structure or border to something else, with the gestured verticals becoming appendages to the black, rather than its support or its frame. The black roughly overextends these lines, furthering the dynamism of the arch. The lines are not boundaries. They force the eye to create the space; it does not come ready-made.

The black is also heavily textured with tones of gray. The texturing creates its own action within the black, giving the lie to an idea of black as a necessarily static field. But the texturing does not create any visual depth within the black. It is all surface. Black is ultimately final; the other colors are left to create the depth below. Daubs of color—green, yellow, blue—proliferate behind the black, appearing in areas where it has been rubbed away. These basic colors are all the more intense for being seen through the screen of the black. They appear as light seen through the thick filter of forest cover. A screen of leaves intensifies the light that comes through; so does the black here, which explodes the color that lies beneath.

This use of one form to introduce and intensify another is something that Jones does frequently. In plate 14, a series of circles laid out on a horizontal line leads the eye to recognize other groups of circles that are less apparent, having been obscured to the point of becoming seemingly random curves that turn out not to be random at all. Or the full circles themselves: they are so clearly a key horizontal factor in the painting. One has to look at them closely, however, to note that they are also positioned to form verticals as well. They are an invitation to look.

More than anything else, plate 14 seems to be about composition, a classic argument of form versus chaos, order versus entropy. The Jones grid is set up roughly, again less as a defining element than a foundation, less a regular grid than a suggestion of order—or a suggestion of disorder, given that the grid lines appear and disappear, as separate elements, varying in strength and definition, creating more zones of activity than structure.

The structure seems to come more from the circles, echoing some of the grid lines, or reinforcing the two strong diagonals that are at the core of the painting's foundation. It's that call and response again, here shapes and lines calling and answering each other, each pointing to the other, creating an intricate composition without sacrificing any dynamism, any willingness to go outside the boundaries. Below the key horizontal, other circles combine with verticals to function as stylized columns, providing the rest of that foundation. There's an architectural integrity here.

The Impressionist color that lies behind is a vivid chaos of yellows, greens, blues, providing a soft and textured layering, a depth. And yet, as deep as the color is, the bouquet that remains is not a memory of a painting of color, but one of structure.

In plate 16, which is significantly smaller than plates 14 and 15, the composition, color, and especially the treatment of space seem more controlled within the bounds of the painting's considerable activity. The background is a profusion of color, an ever-shifting bebop medley, with a commensurate energy. In the foreground, ovals appear with an irregular and offset grid, but here the ovals and the grid function as agents for the presentation of color, not frames so much as statements of potential space. That potential exists to allow for a concentration of color, and the color, as with the large swath of yellow at the center, is an exercise in cutting through paint with a knife. That cutting and working of paint points to the way in which painting can be drawing, with the knife as a stylus, and the color becoming a formation of elemental shape. The black and the yellow oval areas, rough and yet visually complete, anchor the painting in much the same way as the arch does in plate 15.

Jones often layers his paint deeply, adding and subtracting, working toward a moment when the work feels complete. I find plate 13 interesting in relation to the other paintings in this set in that the place where the painting felt complete is close to the canvas. In profuse color and with a grid that has been broken apart into loose geometries, the painting is one of the most elemental in a series of elemental works. Again, that sense of knife as pencil reappears even more clearly. The presence of the canvas, with its attendant texture and roughness, gives the piece a feeling of the immediate, a grittiness that goes against the lightness and intensity of color.

The drawn painting also comes through in plate 6, where the suggested grid is drawn in strong black gestures, foregrounded against fields of yellow and white. The lines move on the canvas, simultaneously flowing and bearing weight. There's a prominent s-curve, a favorite Jones image, with its place as the queen of those lines that both flow and bear weight. The curve has its own compression and its own upward grace. And of course, the s-curve also introduces that ambiguity so common in abstract painting: Is this a figure? Is it a bow to representation? It could be, but does not seem to be so here. S-curves can be hips, two circles can also be breasts, but that identification is secondary, if not tertiary or less, especially when one considers all that actually goes into a figure study (see plate 17, for example), and how few of those elements accompany the simple s-curve.

Ultimately, the Jones contract is about an internal discipline, both the personal discipline of the painter and the structured contradiction of form up against passion. In these paintings, the underlying grid as a nongrid, the interplay of basic geometries, the playful introduction of the s-curve, the force of color—especially black—pushing against line and against color, all are agents of visual struggle. There is a restlessness here, as the carefully composed form is upended and left behind, as color is layered and left behind. And as in a small theater, there's a drama. It's a drama without symbolism or programmatic intent, however. The players are also the roles that they play; the conflict is about itself only. The paint is not about something else; it is playing itself. It is on the canvas to discuss its own existence, and that existence is so fundamental yet so dynamic that it has something to tell us about life, which is itself so much about form, about pushing against the line, about roughness and surprise.

1   *Studio,* 1990

2 *Greek Beach,* 1990

3   *Summer Piece,* 1991

4   *The Balcony*, 1993

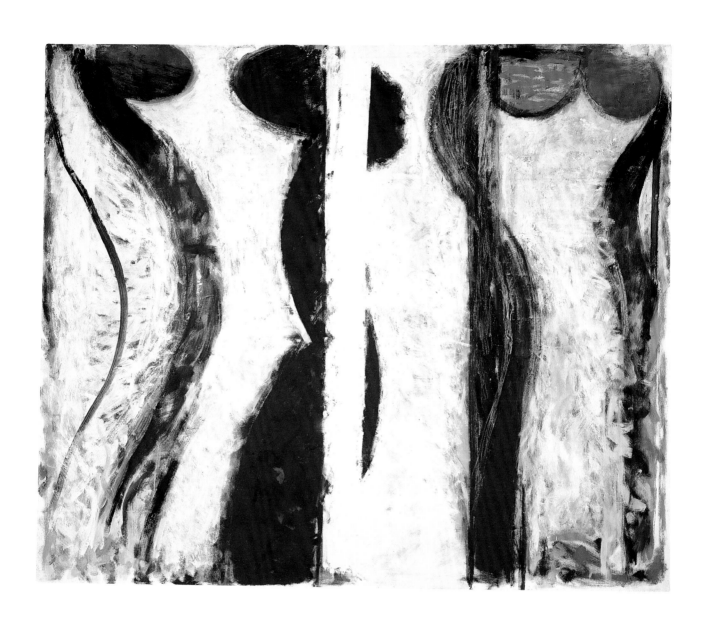

5 *Greek Beach,* 1994

6   *Model and Sculpture, Yellow,* 1996

7   *Portuguese Sweet #7*, 1996

8 *Greek Beach,* 1996

9   *Between the City and the River,* 1996

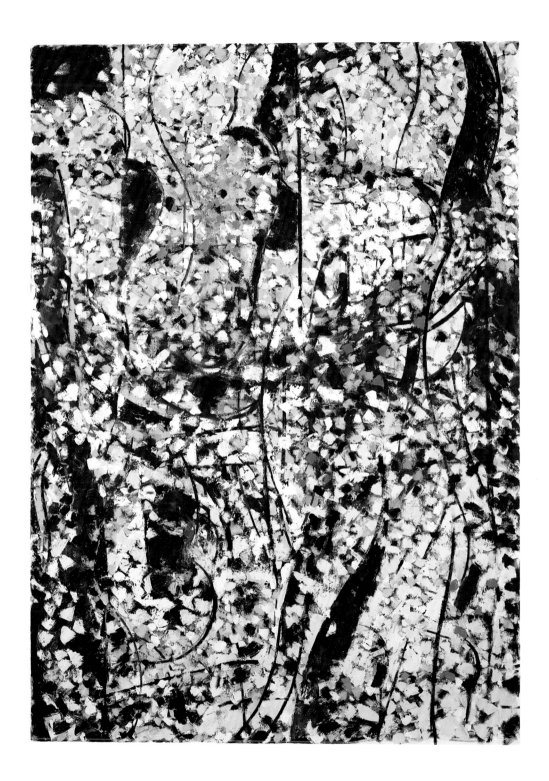

10   *Studio / Yellow*, 1996

11 *Studios*, 1982–97

12   *Untitled*, 1998

13   *Landscape*, 1998

14   *Untitled,* 1999

15 *Untitled*, 1999

16   *Untitled,* 1999

The Immediacy of Lines on Paper

A COUPLE OF YEARS AGO, WHEN I LOOKED AT A SHOW OF DRAW-
ings by Robert Jones, it occurred to me that they might have been drawn by
a student. Not that they weren't good; they were. But more important, they
were fresh and energetic; Jones had kept his beginner's mind.

Jones likes to point out that there is no sharp demarcation between his
drawings and his paintings. To a great extent, that's true: Both travel through
a similar territory, a fundamental investigation of the soul of the human mark
on a surface. Some, even many, of the paintings feel like tremendous gesture
drawings made with paint. And most of the drawings operate on a scale that
runs counter to their small size. Seeing them in reproduction, for example, it
is easy to imagine that they are much larger than they are; they often have a
grand sweep, a large grace.

But the drawings ultimately have their own identity, a way of working
with both a focus and a heightened energy, a way to be in the moment of
making art. They take on an immense amount of weight, they introduce soaring
motion, and they are always examining the architecture of line and shape. They
do so, however, most often within the confines of a few inches.

"It's the immediacy of a drawing that I like," Jones says. "You get results
faster, and you rule out other possibilities, like color." The mode of subtraction
seems critical for him, where one can eliminate the superfluous, like a scientist
or a poet, eliminating or introducing variables at will, sometimes consciously
and sometimes not, all the while keeping an eye on the distance, on the elusive

line. "Line seems to be the most direct and simple way to make an immediate statement. It takes a position, begins to define a space almost immediately."

That line has gone though numerous permutations over the years, as Jones has moved from figurative work into a restless series of experiments: examinations of the geometries of form and tones of gray, the grace of curvature in hundreds of variations, the nature of the calligraphic line, and more recently, hot color, in a series of small, lush watercolors that were the outcome of a stay in Portugal.

Throughout that persistence of change, however, Jones has remained interestingly consistent.

Take the calligraphic work, much of which was done in the 1980s (see plate 30, for example). In it, Jones has made marks on paper that have a calligraphic feel, but the exploration of what seems calligraphic may be more about the experience of moving charcoal across paper. Asian calligraphy is about leaving a trace; it is a pioneering form of abstraction, where the way a line is made is as important as the actual line itself, if not more so. The line is its own process. But calligraphy is liquid; it is done with ink, which leaves a complete and detailed record of that process. Where Jones has made his marks with charcoal, there's a sort of anticalligraphy. In the traces it leaves, charcoal can leave a record of its own process, but more often than not, that record is obscured and disguised. It is the energy in the drawing that surfaces. It's a calligraphy of action, of gesture, not one of artifice and patience.

Those lines that are simultaneously calligraphic and not calligraphic show up elsewhere, in that broader, larger scale, as in plate 43. The size of the piece may not be any greater, but the marks on paper are certainly more massive. The same sensibility applies, though; the line captures the energy in its making. The sweep of the line gives a hint of an action that consumes itself as it sweeps across the page.

Line may be an action; it's also a way to capture a static form: "Geometric forms still interest me as basic forms," Jones says. "They've not been exhausted."

But the line must live on its own, according to its own dynamic. "So much of line becomes light and shade; it becomes the subject and becomes subservient to the form. If those lines become too figurative, only descriptive, it sucks the life out of them, because that sets up the situation where you're looking at a picture of something else. Drawing is often the illustration of something; it *should* be the thing.

"I am not interested in light rolling over the thigh. I'm bored with most descriptive work. Either it's Buick fenders or women's breasts; it all comes from something. When it becomes only a figure drawing, it doesn't have that double life . . . unless it has that architectural quality, the architecture of the figure on the page. That's what's really exciting.

"I also like accidental lines," he says, "happy accidents, like when I used to see a line that a kid made in the sand, or the line that was left when we once took an old refrigerator off the porch. They're things that I find, and very often they're incredibly beautiful."

Jones moves among materials and themes, restlessly. "You get bored with certain materials," he says. When he works with ink, he prefers brush to pen, where all the work is in the wrist. "At Rhode Island [Rhode Island School of Design, where Jones studied as an undergraduate], they taught calligraphy, especially the chancery hand. I couldn't do it. I prefer the gestural brush or charcoal mark. With that gesture, movement is much the same in all the work: paint, ink, charcoal. It's almost easier to draw the wrong lines with paint than it is with charcoal."

On the other hand, "there are things you can't do in charcoal; you need the fluidity of paint. Paint or ink moves fairly fast, while charcoal has that drag quality to it; it's the difference between a soft pencil and a hard pencil. It's a choice—like chicken or pork; you just do it."

If the work seems awash with ideas, that's because it is. But Jones is not a calculating player; more it's a matter of athletics, of carefully learning how to play a sport, and then forgetting everything you've just learned and simply doing it. Jones recalls the Seattle Seahawk running back Curt Warner talking about a game. As the game went on and Warner got more and more tired, "he would get better and better. He said that he stopped thinking and just played; he seized the opportunity.

"I want the work to be intuitive, intensely visual, and hopefully new for me," Jones says. It's that search for a level of connectedness to the work, the task, that has little to do with conscious thought.

"It's a matter of making space that wasn't there before . . . mostly to break something that becomes too formal. It's very hard to make something you haven't seen before . . . it's hard to be chaotic. But I like not knowing where they will end up; it's that freshness and vitality, that kind of immediacy." Jones talks of the current big band revival, marked by careful re-creation of old styles. "Players are playing the music as someone else played it," he points out. With that, though, you always know how things will turn out.

"You have to force yourself to be untidy, to leave it." Each painting, each drawing, becomes an exploration, without Jones knowing if there will be a good horn solo or not.

Jones likes to paraphrase the late Howard J. Sachs, a Harvard professor, dividing the world into people who care about drawings and people who don't. There's more than a little insight in that split. It's not that individuals cannot in their lives be both kinds of people, but there's a certain way of looking and knowing that drawings represent, and not everyone sees the world that way. I agree with Jones when he maintains that "drawing is undervalued in today's art scene, in education and the marketplace." If all art has elements of being language, Jones sees drawing as something further away: "Drawing needs to be studied like a foreign language. The education process doesn't teach us how to read drawings. You have to look and figure out what a drawing means." It's the simplest means that an artist can use, yet it remains one with which we are the least comfortable.

Perhaps audiences are looking for the most bang for the buck, a sense that the artist is working hard to bring us an artifact, and that's what makes it valuable. Maybe drawing seems too much like fun, like creating a haiku instead of an epic.

One has to think about the haiku, however, to understand what goes into a good drawing: a balancing of words and images, layer upon layer of meaning and discovery, all within a small space, and all appearing as if effortless. It's what has made haiku, even in translation, so timeless, and what makes good drawing so valuable and so difficult to value.

For Bob Jones, it is a life's calling.

17   *Untitled,* 1963–64

18   *Untitled,* 1964

19   *Untitled,* 1965

20 *Untitled*, 1965

21   *Untitled*, 1966

22   *Pharaoh's Blatz*, 1967

23   *Untitled*, 1972

24   *Untitled*, 1974

25   *Untitled*, 1974

26   *Untitled*, 1975

27   *Untitled*, 1977

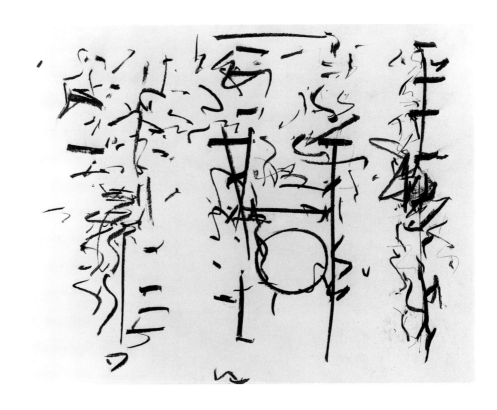

28 *Assisi*, 1978

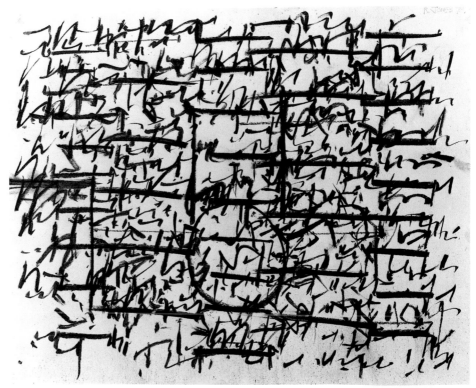

29 *Untitled*, 1978

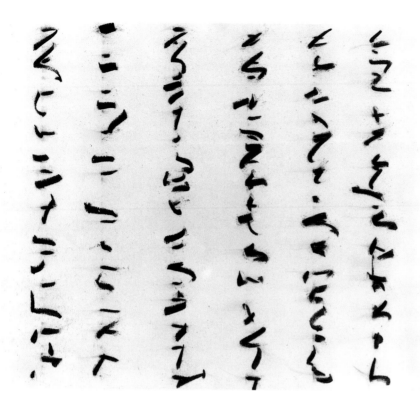

30 *Untitled,* 1978

31 *Untitled,* 1979

32   *Untitled*, 1981

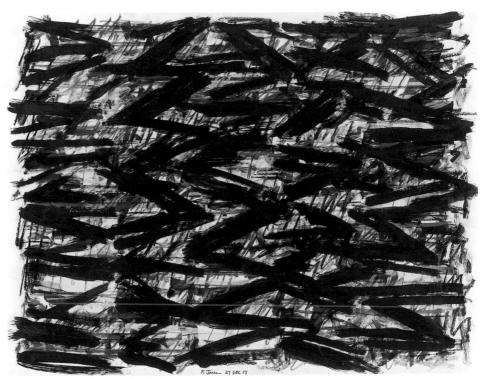

33   *Untitled*, 1983

34   *Untitled*, 1986

35   *Untitled*, 1987

36   *Untitled*, 1987

37   *Untitled*, 1990

38   *Untitled,* 1991

39   *Untitled,* 1992

40   *Untitled,* 1992

41   *Untitled,* 1993

42   *Untitled*, 1993

43   *Untitled,* 1993

44   *Untitled,* 1994

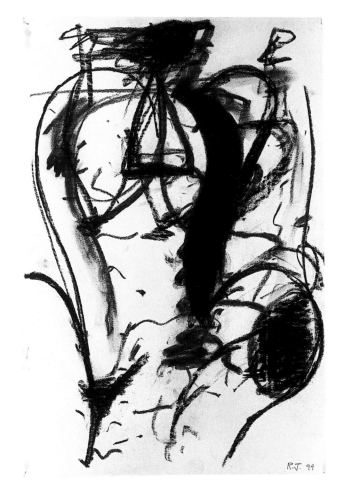

45 *Untitled,* 1994   46 *Untitled,* 1994

47 *Untitled*, 1995   48 *Untitled*, 1995

49   *Untitled*, 1995   50   *Portuguese Sweet #10*, 1996

51   *Untitled,* 1997

52   *Untitled,* 1997

53   *Untitled*, 1997

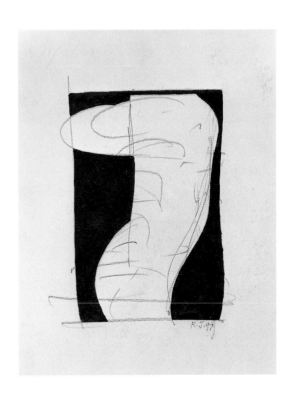

54   *Untitled*, 1997

55   *Untitled*, 1998

56   *Untitled*, 1998   57   *Untitled*, 1998

58   *Untitled,* 1998

All dimensions are sheet measurements; height precedes width. All objects courtesy Francine Seders Gallery, Seattle, unless otherwise indicated.

1. *Studio,* 1990
   Oil on canvas
   67½ × 87½ inches

2. *Greek Beach,* 1990
   Oil on canvas
   67 × 87 inches

3. *Summer Piece,* 1991
   Oil on canvas
   60 × 72 inches
   Private Collection

4. *The Balcony,* 1993
   Oil on canvas
   60 × 77½ inches
   Collection Microsoft Corporation

5. *Greek Beach,* 1994
   Oil on canvas
   40 × 48 inches
   Private Collection

6. *Model and Sculpture, Yellow,* 1996
   Oil on canvas
   30 × 36 inches

7. *Portuguese Sweet #7,* 1996
   Watercolor on paper
   6½ × 4¾ inches
   Private Collection

8. *Greek Beach,* 1996
   Oil on canvas
   35 × 34 inches
   Private Collection

9. *Between the City and the River,* 1996
   Oil on canvas
   55 × 76½ inches

10. *Studio / Yellow,* 1996
    Oil on canvas
    78 × 56 inches

11. *Studios,* 1982–97
    Oil on canvas
    77¾ × 63¾ inches

12. *Untitled,* 1998
    Oil on canvas
    67 × 54 inches

13. *Landscape,* 1998
    Oil on canvas
    36 × 32 inches

14. *Untitled,* 1999
    Oil on canvas
    66 × 55 inches

15. *Untitled,* 1999
    Oil on canvas
    67¼ × 54¼ inches

16. *Untitled,* 1999
    Oil on canvas
    40¼ × 30 inches

17. *Untitled,* 1963–64
    Graphite on paper
    10⅝ × 14 inches

18. *Untitled,* 1964
    Graphite on paper
    14 × 10¾ inches

19. *Untitled,* 1965
    Charcoal on paper
    30½ × 25½ inches

20. *Untitled,* 1965
    Charcoal on paper
    25½ × 30½ inches

21. *Untitled*, 1966
Acrylic on paper
22½ × 28½ inches

22. *Pharaoh's Blatz*, 1967
Oil on paper
24 × 30 inches

23. *Untitled*, 1972
Charcoal on paper
24 × 30 inches

24. *Untitled*, 1974
Charcoal on paper
24 × 30 inches

25. *Untitled*, 1974
Charcoal on paper
24 × 30 inches

26. *Untitled*, 1975
Charcoal on paper
24 × 30 inches

27. *Untitled*, 1977
Charcoal on paper
24 × 30 inches

28. *Assisi*, 1978
Charcoal on paper
17½ × 22½ inches

29. *Untitled*, 1978
Charcoal on paper
19 × 24 inches

30. *Untitled*, 1978
Charcoal on paper
15 × 19 inches

31. *Untitled*, 1979
Pastel and charcoal on paper
15 × 18 inches

32. *Untitled*, 1981
Ink, pastel, and charcoal on paper
15 × 19 inches

33. *Untitled*, 1983
Pastel, ink, and charcoal on paper
22½ × 30 inches

34. *Untitled*, 1986
Oil, acrylic, charcoal, pastel, and collage
on paper
22 × 32½ inches

35. *Untitled*, 1987
Oil on paper
20 × 25¼ inches

36. *Untitled*, 1987
Oil on paper
16 × 20 inches

37. *Untitled*, 1990
Oil on board
12½ × 19½ inches

38. *Untitled*, 1991
Graphite on paper
6 × 8 inches

39. *Untitled*, 1992
Ink on paper
2½ × 3¾ inches

40. *Untitled*, 1992
Oil on paper
22 × 30 inches

41. *Untitled*, 1993
Oil on paper
19 × 30 inches

42. *Untitled*, 1993
Acrylic on paper
15 × 19 inches
Private Collection

43. *Untitled*, 1993
Oil on paper
15 × 17 inches

44. *Untitled*, 1994
Oil on paper
22 × 30 inches

45. *Untitled*, 1994
Charcoal on paper
22 × 15 inches

46. *Untitled*, 1994
Ink on paper
11 × 8½ inches

47. *Untitled*, 1995
Graphite and collage on paper
11 × 7½ inches

48. *Untitled*, 1995
Graphite on paper
8½ × 6 inches
Private Collection

49. *Untitled*, 1995
Collage and graphite on paper
8½ × 5 inches

50. *Portuguese Sweet #10*, 1996
Watercolor on paper
7½ × 4½ inches
Private Collection

51. *Untitled*, 1997
Graphite, ink, and collage on paper
8¼ × 8½ inches

52. *Untitled*, 1997
Ink, graphite, and collage on paper
8½ × 10¾ inches

53. *Untitled*, 1997
Ink and graphite on paper
8½ × 8⅛ inches

54. *Untitled*, 1997
Ink and graphite on paper
9½ × 8¼ inches

55. *Untitled*, 1998
Ink and graphite on paper
10 × 6¾ inches

56. *Untitled*, 1998
Ink and charcoal on paper
8½ × 6½ inches

57. *Untitled*, 1998
Ink and graphite on paper
10¾ × 7¼ inches

58. *Untitled*, 1998
Ink, watercolor, and graphite on paper
7 × 6 inches

ROBERT C. JONES

Born 1930, West Hartford, Connecticut

EDUCATION

1957–59   M.S., Rhode Island School of Design

1952   Hans Hofmann, Summer School

1950–53   B.F.A., Rhode Island School of Design

1948–50   Kenyon College, Gambier, Ohio

HONORS

1990   Western States Arts Federation/ National Endowment for the Arts Fellowship

SELECTED SOLO EXHIBITIONS

1999   *Robert C. Jones Drawings & Paintings,* Pierce College, Tacoma

    Francine Seders Gallery, Seattle (also 1998, 1997, 1996, 1993, 1991, 1988, 1985, 1982, 1980, 1979, 1975, 1972, 1970)

1990   Whatcom Museum of History and Art, Bellingham, Washington

1987   *Documents Northwest,* Seattle Art Museum

1984   Art Center Gallery, Seattle Pacific University

1982   Tacoma Art Museum

    Oregon State University, Corvallis

1965   University of Montana, Missoula

    Scott Galleries, Seattle

SELECTED GROUP EXHIBITIONS

1997   *Square Painting/Plane Painting,* curated by Lauri Chambers, CoCA, Seattle

1995   *Northwest Art: Shaped by the Spirit, Shaped by the Hand,* Museum of Northwest Art, La Conner, Washington

Washington: 100 Years, 100 Paintings,
Bellevue Art Museum, Bellevue,
Washington

1994   *Tacoma Art Museum: Selections from the
Northwest Collection,* Seafirst Gallery,
Seattle

Drawings, Kirkland Arts Center,
Kirkland, Washington

1991   *Paintings by Four WESTAF Fellowship
Recipients,* The Nevada Museum of
Art, Reno

*Academy-Institute Invitational Exhibition of
Painting and Sculpture,* American
Academy and Institute of Arts and
Letters, New York

1989   *100 Years of Washington Art,* Tacoma Art
Museum

Decade of Abstraction 1979–1989,
A Bumbershoot Visual Arts Exhibi-
tion, curated by Matthew Kangas,
Seattle Center

1987   *Focus: Seattle,* San Jose Museum of Art,
San Jose, California

1986   *Northwest Impressions: Works on Paper,*
Henry Art Gallery, University of
Washington, Seattle

10/40 Anniversary Exhibition, Bellevue
Art Museum, Bellevue, Washington

1985   *Seattle Painting 1925–1985,*
Bumberbiennale, Seattle Center

1984   *SIZE,* Bumberbiennale, Seattle Center

1983   *Contemporary Seattle Art of the 1980's,*
Bellevue Art Museum, Bellevue,
Washington

1981   *Seattle Drawings: An Invitational Exhibition,*
Art Center Gallery, Seattle Pacific
University

The Mind's Eye: Expressionism, Henry Art
Gallery, University of Washington,
Seattle

1977   *Northwest '77,* Seattle Art Museum

Robert C. Jones, Fay Jones, Adlai Steven-
son Library, University of California,
Santa Cruz

1971   *Drawings U.S.A.,* Saint Paul Museum,
Saint Paul

1967   *The West—80 Contemporaries,* University
of Arizona, Tucson

1965   *Far West Regional Exhibition of Art Across
America,* San Francisco Museum
of Art

1963   *82nd Annual Exhibition,* San Francisco
Museum of Art

Younger Washington Artists, Henry Art
Gallery, University of Washington,
Seattle

1962   *175th Annual Exhibition of American
Painting and Sculpture,* Pennsylvania
Academy of the Fine Arts,
Philadelphia

PUBLIC AND CORPORATE COLLECTIONS:

The Lakes Club, Bellevue, Washington
Microsoft Corporation, Redmond,
    Washington
Municipal Collection, Seattle
Safeco Corporation, Seattle
SeaFirst Bank, Seattle
Seattle City Light
Stoel, Rives, Boley, Jones and Grey, Seattle
University of Washington, Seattle
Weyerhaeuser Company, Auburn,
    Washington

Library of Congress Catalog Card
Number: 99-73875
ISBN: 0-295-97921-6

Distributed by
University of Washington Press
P.O. Box 50096
Seattle, Washington 98145

Printed by C & C Offset Printing Co., Ltd.,
Hong Kong

Front cover: *Model and Sculpture, Yellow*, 1996
(plate 6)
Back cover: *Model and Sculpture, Yellow*, 1996
(plate 6, detail)
Frontispiece: *Untitled*, 1965 (plate 19)

Designed by Susan E. Kelly
Produced by Marquand Books, Inc., Seattle

All photos by Spike Mafford except as
indicated:
John Granen: Portrait of the artist, 1998,
page 3
Eduardo Calderón: plates 2–5, 7, 8, 38–42,
44–50
Preston Wadley: plate 35